RUTH RICHARDS, a former New Yorker, is a yoga teacher in Phoenix, Arizona. She has also taught in hospitals and in a juvenile girl's home and has worked with church and drug rehabilitation groups. She is co-author of YOGA FOR CHILDREN, a somewhat more junior book than this one.

JOY ABRAMS earned her B.A. in early childhood education and her M.A. in elementary education and is presently earning a second M.A. in learning disabilities. She has taught first grade and kindergarten and she has worked with youngsters with learning disabilities. Ms. Abrams lives in Phoenix with her husband and children, all of whom do yoga.

SANDRA E. CASE is doing graduate in art at Arizona State University.

🧘 Let's Do Yoga

🪷 Ruth Richards and Joy Abrams

Let's Do Yoga

illustrated by
Sandra E. Case

Holt, Rinehart and Winston 🪷 New York

Copyright © 1975 by Holt, Rinehart and Winston, Inc.
All rights reserved including the right to reproduce this book
or portions thereof in any form.
Published simultaneously in Canada by Holt, Rinehart and Winston
of Canada, Limited.
Designed by Victoria Gomez
Printed in the United States of America

Library of Congress Cataloging in Publication Data

Richards, Ruth.
   Let's do yoga.

   SUMMARY: An introduction to simple yoga postures designed
to stretch and tone the muscles, to keep the spine and
joints limber, and to instruct in proper breathing methods.
   1. Yoga, Hatha—Juvenile literature. [1. Yoga]
I. Abrams, Joy, joint author. II. Case, Sandra E.
ill. III. Title.
RA781.7.R52   613.7'042   74-22199
ISBN 0-03-014006-4

ॐ introduction

GOOD HEALTH HABITS

Good habits are formed in early childhood, and it is our intention with this book to encourage young children in the practice of physical fitness. Learning these simple yoga postures will promote a strong and healthy body and an alert mind. Yoga is a science that is centuries old, and as a form of physical culture it remains unsurpassed. Although there are many branches of yoga, some dealing with the spiritual and mental sides, we deal here with the physical side of yoga, or *Hatha Yoga,* as it is called.

HATHA YOGA

Hatha yoga is a series of postures or *asanas* designed to stretch and tone the muscles, to keep the spine and joints limber and to instruct in the proper breathing methods. All postures are accomplished by slow and easy movement, never forcing or straining the body. The relaxation part of yoga sets it apart from other forms of physical exercise. The relaxation process recaptures the energy used in doing the postures and allows one to finish refreshed and alert.

FOR SCHOOLTEACHERS

It has been Joy Abrams' experience, in teaching children who are hyperkinetic and those with visual-perception difficulties, that they benefited from a few minutes of yoga breathing before the class. It calmed the children and facilitated clearer thinking on their part. Generally speaking, children with learning disabilities also have problems with coordination. The balance and reverse postures helped these children and gave them confidence.

Yoga can also be integrated with other curriculum areas at the primary level. Here are a few ideas which teachers have tried and found helpful.

Health
- What are the different ways we can keep our bodies fit?
- What are the foods yogis eat daily, in order to maintain good health?

Social Studies
- A visit to a yoga studio.
- A visit to the classroom by a yoga instructor, for discussing healthful modes of living.

Language and Arts
- Experience charts.
- Where do yogis live?
- What do they eat?
- How do they dress?

Math
- Compare prices of health foods yogis eat with the prices of other foods, making charts of comparison. For example: Are raw almonds more expensive than normally processed almonds?

Music and Dance
- Create your own slow-moving dance, combining your favorite yoga postures from this book.

A daily yoga routine can bring a calm and happy atmosphere into the classroom for children and teacher.

FOR EVERYONE

The intentions of this book are broader than that, however. We seek to promote for all children sounder health, a more relaxed disposition and a happier future. For yoga can be practiced anyplace. The postures may be done indoors or outdoors, at home on the floor, at school in the gym or in any appropriate room. Whether at the beach or in the back yard, whether on a beach towel, a straw mat or the floor, each child should have his or her own little space with enough room to move around in. A leotard or any loose clothing without restrictions or belts may be worn.

HOW TO PRACTICE
1. Pretend you are alone in the room. There is no competition in yoga. Practice to the best of your ability, without concern for what others are doing.
2. Move slowly, never forcing or straining the body, but with the intention of improving each posture gradually.
3. When moving back or forward, or when coming up from a down position, move with the spine, keeping the head, neck and spine in a straight line.
4. With practice the breathing postures will become natural; you will be exchanging an old habit for a new one.
5. Wait at least an hour after a meal before practicing.

RELAXATION
Whenever relaxation is called for in a posture, rest for a few seconds.

- A slow count of ten is suggested.
- When you are standing, close the eyes, relax the shoulders and let the arms hang loosely at the sides.
- When you are seated, close the eyes, rest hands lightly on the knees, keep the back straight and have the body free of tension.
- When lying on the stomach, keep arms at the sides, away from the body, feet slightly apart, body loose and limp, and cheek on the floor.

And now LET'S DO YOGA.

Dedicated to Ray and Carol with love. *Ruth Richards*

To Mom, Dad and Ken for their encouragement;
to Nancy and David for their inspiration. *Joy Abrams*

🕉 postures

Easy Pose · Perfect Posture · Rock Pose

Cleansing Breath · Proper Breathing · Full Breath

Pendulum · Triangle · Tree

Butterfly · Lotus · Dwarf

Figure Eight Neck Roll · Turtle · Clock

Modified Headstand · Modified Tripod Headstand

Candle · Plough · Fish

Arch · Windmill · Bridge

Cobra · Boat · Bow

Rocking · Complete Relaxation

ॐ easy pose

Easy Pose when practiced will encourage a straight and supple spine. As you sit, keep head, neck and trunk in a straight line.

Sit with the back straight, and legs forward.

Bend the right knee and place the right foot under the left thigh.

Bring the left foot in to touch the right leg.

Sit quietly with hands resting on the knees.

ॐ perfect posture

Perfect Posture. The spine is in perfect alignment when seated in this posture.

Sit with the back straight and legs forward.

Bend the left knee and place the left foot under the right thigh.

Bring the right foot in, and place it on top of the left leg.

Sit quietly with hands resting on the knees.

🪷 rock pose

Rock Pose, stretching the thighs and bending the knees, will help to keep the joints limber.

Kneel down, keeping the back straight.

Sit back on the heels, with the toes uncurled.

Place the hands on the knees, and sit quietly.

❦ cleansing breath

Cleansing Breath is used to expel all the stale air from the lungs. Inhale through the nose, exhale through the mouth.

Sit in the Easy Pose.

In three easy stages, sniff the air, through the nose. Sniff, sniff, sniff.

Now, pull the stomach in, and at the same time breathe out with a whistle, until all the air is out.

Repeat this three times.

ꙮ proper breathing

Proper Breathing is a technique for diaphragm breathing, which is the correct way to breathe. Inhale and exhale through the nose.

Sit in the Rock Pose.

Place the right hand on the stomach.

Breathe in through the nose, letting the stomach come out. Feel it rise.

Breathe out through the nose, pulling the stomach in. Feel it go down.

Repeat this three times.

🪷 full breath

Full Breath, a smooth, deep, full breathing, brings a maximum of oxygen into the body to clear the mind and give more energy. Inhale and exhale through the nose.

Stand up gracefully.

At the same time: breathe in through the nose, letting the stomach out, and lift the arms sideways, high over the head.

At the same time: breathe out through the nose, pulling the stomach in, and lower the arms slowly to the sides.

Repeat this three times.

❀ pendulum

Pendulum is a gentle limbering-up posture to relax the upper torso.

Stand straight with the feet wide apart.

Breathe in, lifting the arms sideways, up over the head.

Now bend at the waist, bringing the arms and upper torso forward, to hang down relaxed.
Breathe out.

Swing slowly with the waist, letting the arms swing back and forth from side to side.
Do this five or six times.
STOP.

Rise up slowly, slowly, slowly until the back is straight.

RELAX.

❧ triangle

Triangle gives a good stretch to the legs, the back and the arms.

Stand straight with the feet wide apart.

At the same time: breathe in and raise the arms sideways to shoulder height.

Keeping the right arm up, bend slowly to the left and touch the left foot.

Keeping the head straight, breathe out and bring the right arm over the head. The elbow is straight.

With straight legs and arms, hold this posture for a count of six.

Straighten up slowly.
Repeat bending to the right side.

Repeat the full posture, left and right, once more.

RELAX.

❦ tree

Tree is a balance posture for control. Concentrating on one spot helps you to hold your balance.

Stand straight with the feet close together.

Put the weight of the body on the right side.

Bend the left knee, take the left foot in both hands and place foot on top of the right thigh.

Now lift the arms up over head, touch palms together and, looking straight ahead, stand straight and still for a count of six.

Bring the left foot down gracefully.

Repeat the posture standing on the left leg.

RELAX.

🦋 butterfly

Butterfly gives a good stretch to the thigh muscles and to the knees. Making circles with the toes helps to limber up the ankles.

Sit with the back straight and legs out in front.

Lift the right leg and make circles with the toes. Put the leg down.

Lift the left leg and make circles with the toes. Put the leg down.

Now bring the bottoms of the feet together, and clasp the hands under the feet.

Move the knees up and down slowly, six times.

Remove the hands, straighten the legs.

RELAX.

🪷 lotus

Lotus, a classic yoga posture, will help to keep hip joints and legs limber.

Sit with a straight back and legs out in front.

Bend the right knee and take the right foot in both hands.

Turn the foot so that the bottom part is facing up.
Place the right foot on the left thigh.

Bend the left leg, take the left foot in both hands and place it on the right thigh.

You are sitting in the Lotus posture. Sit quietly for a count of ten.

To come out, gently lift first one leg off the thigh, then the other, and bring both legs out in front of you.

Now try it on the other side, bringing up the left foot first.

🕉 dwarf

Dwarf, a more advanced posture involving hip joints, knees and ankles, develops balance and control.

Sit straight, legs out in front.

Bend the right knee and take the right foot in both hands. Place it high on top of the left thigh.

Place the left foot flat on the floor. Pull it in close.

Pressing the hands down on either side of yourself for balance, bring the body up to rest on the right knee and left foot.

Place hands together at the chest and balance for a count of ten.

To come out; first place hands on the floor and sit back slowly. Lift the right foot off the left thigh and straighten out both legs.

Now try it on the opposite side, placing the left foot high on the right thigh.

RELAX.

🪷 figure eight neck roll

Figure Eight Neck Roll is a slow, easy movement to rid the neck of stiffness and tension.

Sit in the Easy Pose, back straight and chin tucked in.

Let the head hang forward, chin on the chest.

Now lift the head, moving it slowly over the right shoulder, then to the back, then back down to the chest.

Without stopping, lift the head, moving it slowly up over the left shoulder, then to the back, then back down to the chest.

Repeat this three times.

🪷 turtle

Turtle stretches and tones the neck muscles.

Sit in the Easy Pose, with the back straight.

Place the right hand high on the chest.

Holding the chest back, stretch the neck forward. Hold for a count of four.

Now relax the neck and bring it back, so that back and neck are in a straight line.

Repeat this three times.

❀ clock

Clock is an exercise for the eye muscles.

Sit with a straight back
in the Easy Pose.

Pretend that the nose is attached
to a great big clock.
Keep the head still and slowly move
only the eyes.

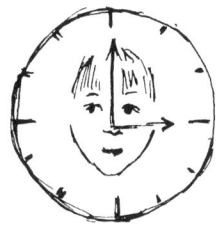

First to twelve.

Then to three.

Down to six.

Up to nine.

Back to twelve.

Now close the eyes for a few seconds to rest them.

Repeat this in the opposite direction, 12-9-6-3-12.

ॐ modified headstand

Modified Headstand is an aid in bringing oxygen to the brain and promotes clear thinking.

Kneel down.

Interlock the fingers and place them on the floor, leaning on the elbows.

Bring the head down and place the back of the head between your hands.

Raise up on the toes, and hold this position for a count of ten.

To come out, put the knees on the floor, and keeping the head down, sit back on the heels. Relax in this position for a count of ten.

Sit up slowly.

RELAX.

❧ modified tripod headstand

Modified Tripod Headstand is a more advanced posture. Control is important here, as the knees are brought down slowly.

Kneel down and place the top of the head on the floor.

Place the hands on either side, a shoulder's width apart, and back far enough to see the fingers.

Come up on the toes and walk in toward the hands.

Place the right knee on the right elbow.

Place the left knee on the left elbow. Hold for a count of ten.

To come out, slowly and with control bring one foot at a time to the floor. Keeping the head down, slowly sit back on the heels.

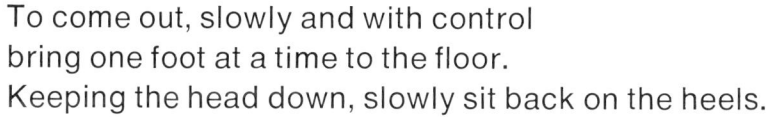

Relax in this position for a count of ten.

🕉 candle

Candle is a posture reversing the pull of gravity. The weight of the body is on the shoulders, strengthening this area.

Lie flat on your back.
Tuck in the shoulder blades.
Legs straight, feet together.

Support the back with both hands and raise both legs slowly.

Work the hands up the back until they are at the shoulder blades. Straighten back and legs.

Hold for a count of ten.

To come out, bend the knees to the forehead and bring the arms to the sides.

Arch the neck back and roll out slowly, keeping the head on the floor.

Slowly lower the legs to the floor.

RELAX.

ॐ plough

Plough gives a complete stretch to the spine and legs.

Lie flat on the back, arms at the sides, palms pressing against the floor.

Keeping the knees straight, lift the legs, then the hips, bending the back until the toes touch the floor behind the head.

Bring the arms back and touch the toes. Hold for a count of ten.

To come out, bend the knees to the forehead.
Roll out slowly, arching the neck back, keeping the head on the floor.

Slowly lower the legs to the floor.

RELAX.

🪷 fish

Fish posture always follows the Candle and Plough, to stretch the neck and spine in the opposite direction.

Lie on the back, legs together, feet up.

Place the hands under the hips, palms against the floor.

Lean on the elbows and raise the chest, bending the head back until the top of it rests on the floor. Hold for a count of six.

To come out, slowly straighten neck, and head, lower back to the floor, bring arms to the sides.

RELAX.

ॐ arch

Arch aids in keeping the back limber.

Lie on the back, knees bent and feet close in.

Reach forward with both hands and take hold of the ankles.

At the same time: inhale and arch the back, raising it up, but keeping the head and shoulders on the floor. Hold for a count of six.

Exhale and come down slowly, first the upper back, then the waist, then the lower back.

Let the feet slide forward to straighten the legs.

RELAX.

ॐ windmill

Windmill is a posture for control in which the stomach muscles play a large part.

Lie flat on the back, arms at the sides.

Raise both legs slowly and bring both hands up to support the hips.

Bend the knees and bring the right leg forward until the toe touches the floor.

As you bring the left leg forward to touch the floor, start lifting the right leg.

Have only one foot touching the floor at a time.

Go up and down a few times.

To come out, bring both feet to the floor, lower the back slowly and straighten the legs.

RELAX.

🪷 bridge

Bridge gives a complete stretch to the back and the slow coming out of it massages the spine.

Lie flat on the floor, legs apart.

Bend the knees, bringing the feet close to the body.

Place the hands under the waist, and lift the body, using the elbows for support.

Now up on the toes.
Hold for a count of ten.

To come out, bring the hands to the sides.
Remaining on the toes, lower the back slowly, slowly, slowly to the floor.

Slide the feet forward, straighten the legs.

RELAX.

🕉 cobra

Cobra strengthens the neck and chest muscles and stimulates circulation in the lower back.

Lie face down, forehead on the floor, arms at the sides, feet together.

Lift head and chest, moving hands forward, fingers facing but not touching.

Inhale, lean on the hands, bend back at the waist, keeping the hips on the floor.

With head arched back and eyes open, look up.
—hold for a count of six.

To come down, exhale and slowly lower first the waist.
When the chest touches the floor, bring the arms to the sides.

Lower the forehead to the floor, and rest on your cheek.

RELAX.

🙏 boat

Boat, with the arms and legs forming the shape of a boat, is a posture for the back.

Lie face down, arms stretched forward, feet together.

At the same time: inhale and raise arms, head and legs as high as you can, until you are resting on the stomach.
Hold for a count of six.

Exhale and slowly lower arms, head and legs to the floor.

RELAX.

🕉 bow

Bow gives the combined effect of Cobra and Boat, toning all the muscles of the back.

Lie flat on the stomach,
chin on the floor.
Bend the knees, bringing the feet up.

Reach back and take hold
of the ankles.

At the same time: breathe in,
lift up the chest and pull the
legs up.
Breathe out.
Hold for a count of six.

To come out, still holding the ankles
lower the thighs to the floor.
Lower head to the floor.

Release ankles and lower the legs.
Rest your cheek on the floor.

RELAX.

ॐ rocking

Rocking is practiced in a slow and easy way.

Sit with a straight back.
Knees are bent.

Lean forward and hold the
legs under the knees.

Feel loose and relaxed.

Still holding the legs,
rock back and forward,
back and forward.

Rock back and forward for as
long as you please, all slow
and easy.

RELAX.

ॐ complete relaxation

Complete Relaxation is essential after practicing yoga. It allows you to regain the energy you have used, and to feel refreshed and renewed. Remain in this position for three to five minutes.

Lie on the back with the eyes closed.
Legs are forward, feet apart.
Arms are resting comfortably at the sides,
away from the body.

Relax the legs and let them feel light.
Relax the arms and let them feel light.
Relax the body until it feels light.
Relax the scalp, the eyes, the ears and the mouth.

Now imagine yourself to be a light, fluffy cloud, floating in a beautiful blue sky.

🕉 about the authors

Ruth Richards, a former New Yorker, is a yoga teacher in Phoenix, Arizona. She has also taught in hospitals and in a juvenile girl's home and has worked with church and drug rehabilitation groups. She is co-author of *Yoga for Children,* a somewhat more junior book than this one.

Joy Abrams earned her B.A. in early childhood education and her M.A. in elementary education and is presently earning a second M.A. in learning disabilities. She has taught first grade and kindergarten and she has worked with youngsters with learning disabilities. Ms. Abrams lives in Phoenix with her husband and children, all of whom do yoga.

🕉 about the artist

Sandra E. Case is doing graduate work in art at Arizona State University.

🕉 about the book

The book is set in Helvetica typeface and illustrated with halftone drawings. The book is printed by offset.